# Double Your Income

## How Real Estate Agents Can Make More Money by Doing Less

By Glenn McQueenie

Copyright © 2014 Glenn McQueenie
All rights reserved.
ISBN-10: 1503016838
ISBN-13: 978-1503016835

# Here's What's Inside...

5 **Introduction**

7 **Double Your Income!**

9 **Why Don't More Real Estate Agents Make Great Money...**

11 **The Secret Blueprint New Agents Are Missing...**

14 **Why the Riches Are in the Niches...**

19 **Why You Should Treat Every Lead as Your Best Friend...**

23 **Why Most Agents Give up Way Too Soon...**

29 **Why Agents Need to Spend 80% of Their Time Focusing on the next Two Clients Most Likely to Buy or Sell...**

30 **How Agents Hit Their Annual Goals...**

30 **Why the 4:1 Ratio of Current Book of Business to Written Transactions Is Key...**

35 **The Secret to Successful Open Houses...**

38 **Why Offering a Free Orientation Tour Works...**

41 **How to Use Geographic Farming to Double Your Income...**

- 45 **How to Take the Stress and Worry out of Real Estate...**
- 49 **Why Agents Should Spend 80% of Their Time Doing What They Love...**
- 51 **The Mistakes to Avoid When Trying to Double Your Income...**
- 54 **What Sellers Really Want from a Real Estate Agent...**
- 56 **What Buyers Really Want from a Real Estate Agent...**
- 57 **How to Turn 1 Listing into 4 Additional Transactions...**
- 60 **How to Get More Referrals from "Referral Chaining"...**
- 62 **Start Selling Real Estate for The "Hugs"...**
- 64 **Here's How to Double Your Income While Working Less...**
- 66 **About the Author**

# Introduction

Double Your Income!
October 2014


I often get asked why some agents seem to close so many deals yet others are just scraping by with only the occasional deal. Even if you only practice real estate part time, this book will include time tested strategies you can employ to ensure a steady stream of income for your real estate business.

These are the exact same strategies I've been sharing for years with agents all over North America with great success. I include proven strategies such as how to turn 1 listing into 4 commission checks; my Secret Blueprint new agents are missing in their real estate practice, which walks you through how to Double Your Income; my secret to successful open houses and why offering a free orientation tour is so effective.

I've found with most agents, they believe they know how to do the business of real estate really well. A more effective methodology and coaching is often the only thing separating the top producers from those who are thinking about leaving the business due to lack of consistent income.

What follows is the transcript where I share with you how I train agents to double their income by working smarter not harder.

Enjoy the Book!

I hope this book educates you on how successful agents get better results and encourages you to change the way you run your real estate business and double your income.

To Your Success!

*Glenn McQueenie*

# Double Your Income!

**Susan:** Good afternoon. This is Susan Austin and I'm excited to be with Glenn McQueenie. Glenn is going to be sharing with us his thoughts and ideas on how real estate agents can make more money by doing less. Welcome Glenn.

**Glenn:** Thanks, Susan.

**Susan:** Let's start off with why you want to write this book?

**Glenn:** I just started getting angry watching so many people come into the real estate business and not learn the proper skills, models and systems to be successful. Watching them after about 6 months or a year, starting to run out of money or they have already run out of money. More importantly, they start to lose the support from their family and they start going into a panic. It has been my experience the more you want a transaction in real estate the less you are going to get it. In fact the opposite is true. The more transactions you have coming in the easier the rest of them all come and fall in your lap.

Many people come into this business because the entry cost to the real estate industry is relatively low compared to any other business. A lot of them get into this business because all of their friends, family and colleagues in other industries have said, "Oh, you will make a great real estate agent. You're going to be awesome and I will use you for sure." I think from the outside our industry looks really easy. They can all figure out what 3% of that purchase price is and go,

"Wow, I just have to sell a couple of homes and I can make a whole lot of money." I believe some people think, "Hey, I like people. I really love houses. How tough can it be? It looks so easy to me."

# Why Don't More Real Estate Agents Make Great Money...

**Susan:** The agents who are coming into the business, why are they having such a hard time? Why do they have a hard time making the good money other agents are making?

**Glenn:** After they take their courses and they complete their licenses they sign up with a brokerage, and they are pretty surprised to realize most brokerages will just take them aboard. It's not like they have to interview for it. Then they start getting busy because a lot of brokerages might even say," Oh, we have great training. Don't worry we'll take good care of you." The fact is most brokerages don't take care of them. You're on your own. The statistics speak for themselves. In the Toronto real estate board we have 41,000 agents and out of the 41,000, 25% don't sell a house a year, and 23% of them, which is almost 9,000 of those agents, only sell one home in a year.

In fact, when I looked really deep into the stats I realized a total of 77% of the agents on the Toronto Real Estate Board sell 6 homes or less a year. In Toronto our average commission is $10,000, which is higher than most places across North America, but if you take 6 times $10,000 that's $60,000. But out of that they have to pay their own expenses, phone, gas, brokerage fees and maybe they are going to be left with $30,000. Then they pay some tax and maybe they are left with $20,000. Under $20,000 is really what 77% of the agents have to live on.

**Susan:** This would be pretty disillusioning then?

**Glenn:** Yeah, it's tough to live on that little amount of money, right? The challenge is that it actually takes great coaching and training in your first 1 to 3 years full time in this business to really get the essence of how it really works. The challenge is most of them will run out of money and then they run out of time. In fact I know probably 70% to 80% of people who get their real estate license are out of the business within two years. The interesting thing is if you look at most Real Estate boards and licensing programs, all of the money is front loaded. They want their money upfront. It's not like, "Oh pay us when you sell your first house," because they know statistically most of them aren't going to be doing that. They have to pay their dues, their licensing costs, all their fees and a lot of the insurance programs usually upfront.

It's sad because the fact is that they all come into the business ready to work hard and get going, but the challenge is they don't get the secret blueprint of how to make money in this business. They come into an office and they walk up to one agent and say, "How do you do it?" They say, "Oh I make all my money from open houses." Then they will run out and try to duplicate that, but they don't have the same experience, right? Or the next agent says, "Oh, I only do internet marketing and oh boy, I do 3 to 4 houses a month." They go sign up for that and start paying for leads upfront. Or you've got to do it through buyer seminars or geographic farming. What happens is they spend their first year or two chasing the shiny object of what other people in the industry might have been doing for 15 or 20 years, but they just don't have the skills, models or systems to come in and do it.

# The Secret Blueprint New Agents Are Missing...

**Susan:** There are agents who make a great living selling homes and are doing quite well though, right?

**Glenn:** Yes! That's really why I think once you can double your income in real estate you'll actually find the secret that you don't work any harder you in fact, work less. You get more time off and at the same time you can build wealth and security for yourself and your family. My message is also for the agents who have been in the business for maybe 3 to 5 years or 3 to 10 years and maybe they got up to $50,000 or maybe up to $80,000 to $100,000, and maybe they can't seem to get higher than that. They don't understand that that was the hardest part of this business, to make the first $50,000 or the first $100,000. Things actually get easier once you understand the secret and start putting some basic models and systems into your business.

**Susan:** So you're not saying to double your income, just work twice as hard?

**Glenn:** No, I have been doing this for over 25 years and I have probably spent over $1,000,000, maybe $1,500,000, on my own teaching, coaching and training over that time, learning from the best people all across North America. I think what I have really discovered is the secret is not working harder, it's working a lot smarter. This starts with focusing on who is my single target market or who is my niche market.

As I have been running this part of the program at my brokerages with agents, I can actually see just this transformation that starts to happen because they stop running around doing everything but really not doing anything, and they just start focusing on that single niche market, working with clients they love to work with, and the homes they love to work with in the areas they love to work and they find there's actually much more business in there because no one is really planning on dominating that market.

Then what happens is that they start making more money. Their income becomes more predictable. They don't have to go through all the highs and lows of their personal cash flow. They really just start taking more time off and really they can almost get their schedule down to 3 or 5 days a week and they end up doubling or tripling their income.

**Susan:** Realistically, for a fairly young or new agent coming into the business, is it realistic for them to think that they can get to the 6 figure income within a year or two?

**Glenn:** I have taken people right from their first year and gotten them up to $200,000 in income. There is no upper limit if they are willing to work hard and focus on a single target market and follow the formula I share throughout the book. It can happen to anybody and there's no reason why we can't have a lot more agents making a lot more money and having a better life as a result.

In fact, this works for new agents and for people who are stuck in a rut right now. Maybe they've gotten to a certain income point but can't seem to go any higher. Often they have developed a mindset or some habits that are limiting them. There is a whole notion of it takes time for your self-esteem to catch up to your self-worth. What I mean by that is some people think, "Oh, if I could just make $50,000, I would be rich." Then they realize $50,000, isn't really that much money. Then they say, "If I can make $100,000, that would be great." What I found is once they get to $50,000, they will stop working because it's like their belief or mindset system kicks in and they think that's enough money.

What I've learned is that you can never have enough money. It takes a while just for people to move up their own needle and say, "You know what, I think I'm worth $75,000, a year. Or I'm worth a $100,000 a year." The beautiful thing is as you start making more money, it gets a lot easier for your self-esteem and self-worth to catch up because you are leading with your income.

## Why the Riches Are in the Niches...

**Susan:** I love it. Let's talk about this formula you've been hinting at. What do these agents need to understand to be able to double their income?

**Glenn:** The number one thing I would say is just stop being a generalist and start being a specialist who operates in the niche market because we've all heard that term, "the riches are in the niches." I think right now that the microchip and the internet is really designed to help people who are in micro markets who are specialists in niche markets because I don't think anyone in Toronto or anywhere in North America just Googles 'looking for a home in Toronto' because too many searches come up.

They certainly probably won't Google 'looking for an agent in Toronto' because every agent in the world would come up. What they start doing is they start their search on the internet. They do all the background work and try to figure out where they want to be. Then they start selecting neighborhoods and that's where I want them to find me because I'm the expert in that neighborhood or I'm the expert in that niche market. Or if I'm going to be working more on my sphere of influence, I want people to know that Glenn is really good at this market.

Most people buy their first home when they are 25 to 32. Then they sometimes will get married or are already married, and then they move up to their next home between 33 and 40. Then if things are going really well, they start moving from their move up home into the luxury or larger home in their late 40s.

Those are all different micro niche markets that you can choose to work in. I know earlier in my career I just started working with first time buyers because I just loved helping them. Then as my database got older and I got older then they said, "Hey Glenn, can you help us sell our house?"

I started getting way more listings and then would move them up. Now a lot of them are just "move them up" and I move them right up to their luxury home. Or they've got parents who are in big luxury homes or in just larger homes and now they are moving more into a condominium, resort golf area or more into assisted living. You can really pick whatever niche you want to work at, either demographically like that or geographically like where do people move, or what we call psychographically, which is really why people move. I want to move because of that great school. Or I want to move because of the great parks or restaurants that I can walk to.

**Susan:** Do you find that agents are open to picking a niche?

**Glenn:** I think what I found is that people are starting to. If you look at the stats, it's the larger teams or the agents who are doing a higher volume and the large teams are starting to get their unfair share of the market. Then at the other end of the spectrum you have the agent who does one or two deals a year. Maybe they just do this part time. They pick away at a lot of the middle producing agents' listings and sales. The generalist middle agent doing 7 to 15 deals a year is really starting to get hammered because they're just finding that technology moves so quickly, they can't be in two places at one time. Or they just don't have the guts to pick one market, out of fear of missing a lead somewhere else.

When a client finds that house on the internet that you are working with, but you are showing another house, you can't be there. One of the steps I'll talk about is just trying to move your business from an "I" business where you do everything and you are the generalist to moving to a "we" or "they" business where you can start hiring that admin support, marketing support, technology support, showing specialist or buyer's agent.

**Susan:** Do agents feel they will be limited if they pick just one niche?

**Glenn:** Some do, yes, I would say to them you should continue doing the rest of it 20% of the time, and spend 80% of your time in your single niche market. If we get a call to sell a big luxury home, I'm not going to say, "No, I don't do that." For sure run and do it. Or if a friend says my daughter or son is looking for a rental, can you go do that? Of course, we are going to serve them all. Instead of spending 100% of your time running around in different markets and never really establishing a base, what if we can just spend 80% of our time and efforts in one market while still serving those types of requests 20% of the time.

Initially it might start off as I'm 20% in my niche market, 80% running around helping everyone because I don't want to lose any transactions. As your niche market starts to grow, maybe a month later or two months to the next quarter maybe, we move into

30% or 40% in our niche market and 60% still being a generalist. What if after a year, we can just move that needle to where now we're 80% of our time in our target market and 20% just taking the random requests that I get that occur every day.

**Susan:** Perfect. I love that. We are adding to what they are already doing, we are not subtracting. Even though it feels at first look you are restricting them, in truth, you are not.

**Glenn:** Yeah, not at all. What I found is once you can actually start working with that dream client, you start not working with anyone else because they are usually folks who you really like. They are really friendly. It's the type of homes you really like to sell. You love being in that neighborhood or it's the peer group from the golf club or the peer group from the bridge club or whatever interests you. You just want to sell even more of these, because you are very similar to that type of person.

**Susan:** How do you recommend they pick their niche?

**Glenn:** The question becomes, "How do I figure out what my niche market is?" Like "What do I do? I would just maybe say look back on the transactions you've done maybe in the last 12 or 18 months and ask yourself, "Who are the people whom you enjoyed the most?" What did they buy? What house did they sell? What did you like about working with them? What did you like about working in that certain area? That's, I think, the first step. "Who would my dream come true client be, if I could wake up every day and that's all I had to serve?" Then you start designing your lead generation model around how you can get in front of these people. If you like investment properties go to or host Investor Seminars; same for first-time buyers. If you want to help seniors move down to a retirement home, get to know the people that run those homes.

The second way to pick a niche, I got this idea from Dan Sullivan, a Strategic Coach, is you just look back at your five biggest paychecks in the last 18 months and think about who were those clients that gave you those five biggest paychecks? You divide that by five and it will give you a number which is your highest average potential commission check. Does that make sense?

**Susan:** Yes.

**Glenn:** That figure represents where your current training mindset is. Where is my highest average commission? I would argue we should spend more time trying to get higher average commission checks all the time. It takes the same amount of effort to sell a $3 million home as it does to sell a $125,000 home.

# Why You Should Treat Every Lead as Your Best Friend...

**Susan:** Let's say we do find your niche is the middle age group. How do you translate picking a niche into finding them?

**Glenn:** The first step I'd want everyone to do is just figure out what their niche is. Who do they want to serve? Then start thinking about "What's keeping them awake at night right now?" What do they need next? Try to figure out what their next move is and then provide it to them in a great way. I think the first way is that every lead that you ever get from now on, start treating every lead like your best friend?

If my best friend called me up and said, "Glenn, we are thinking about selling our house," I probably wouldn't go over with a 48-slide PowerPoint file and do a full listing presentation. I wouldn't go with a buyer agency contract. I would just go over and be with them for an hour or two and have coffee or beer or a soda or whatever it is, and just figure out what's important to them. For the first 15 minutes we probably wouldn't even talk about real estate.

Every lead I get I want to build rapport because I want to find out what their interests are and because I think that this person could be my next best friend. The way I want to treat my best friend is the way that I want all of the agents to treat every new lead that comes to them. It's a completely different relationship starting from how can I come from contribution and treat you like a best friend rather than I'm not going to waste any time on you. I've got to get you qualified, I have to do all this stuff. That's not even what matters because if you spend all your time at the front trying to qualify somebody and thinking, "Oh, I don't want to waste time with them. They've got to sign these buyer contracts or I'm not going to do or give them anything," I think we just start operating from a scarcity mind instead of just coming from flat out contribution "How can I help you? How can I serve you?"

If you start working with them and you find out that they are not qualified, because you have been treating them as your best friend, they know 400 more people at least. If you can just start treating everyone like your best friend, then I think, even if it doesn't work out with that client, they are going to start sending you lots of referrals because they are going to become a raving fan of your business. I've had some clients I've never done business with, but they have sent me 25 to 30 referrals.

**Susan:** Wow, that's pretty eye opening. The tendency is to think to double our income we need to improve our listing presentations and so we go out and think we have to buy a sophisticated presentation and that's the trick to getting more listings.

**Glenn:** No. What's so interesting, and I love the National Association of Realtors (NAR), NAR does this great profile of buyers and sellers every year and then publishes it. If you go to the NAR website you can buy it and download it. They ask the question of Buyers, "How many agents did you interview before deciding on the agent to work with?" 65% of them interviewed only one agent. One! Half the thing is just show up and you've got about a 7 out of 10 chance of working with the client. Then another 10% worked with two agents and then it got to another 9% worked with 3 agents and finally you had 4% or 5% who worked with 20 agents. In fact, do we know that type of person?

On the listing side it gets really interesting. NAR asked "How many agents did you interview before you chose your listing agent?" Guess what, 70% of them only interviewed one agent. Now it's interesting because in my experience many of the sellers whom I go and present to tell me they are interviewing other people, but maybe that is just because they are trying to say, "Hey, we are not ready yet or we want to meet you and see what is going on," and it gives them an out. The fact is 7 out of 10 interview only one. That's huge.

Just get in front of someone and it's yours to get. If I show up as their best friend, and come from a mindset of how can I help you? How can I be of service to you? That is the secret to lead conversion. It's not tricks or gimmicks. It's not, they say this; I counter back with that, I fire an arrow back at you because you gave me this objection. I think that's selling from the 1980s. It's a dated sales model.

**Susan:** What you are proposing doesn't seem like selling. This is simple relationships.

**Glenn:** I don't really think real estate is selling, I know for sure I have never been able to sell a house to anyone who didn't already want it. Never in my 25 years. I don't know anyone who has. We have 300 agents at our brokerage and as far as I know none of them have either. This whole idea that we can convince someone to buy something that they don't want is just crazy. Why don't we show up; show them what they want; let them choose and let's move on their selling or buying time-line not ours.

I talk to agents and they say things like, "Oh, I really need a deal this month." That's not the universe's problem. It's not your buyer's problem, nor the seller's. That's your problem. What we really need to do is get in front of as many people as we can; treat them as best we can and then 15-20% of everyone we meet will do something in the next 30-90 days and the rest will do something maybe in the next 3 months to 12 months. But, why don't we just show up as if it didn't matter.

The more you are not attached to the transaction, I find people know it. I would argue that if you talk to all of my clients and I have had many over the years, they will say Glenn talked me out of more houses than he ever talked me into. And I think it's a great thing for an agent to tell them no, I don't think that's the right house for you. I think we can do better than this.

**Susan:** Very well said.

# Why Most Agents Give up Way Too Soon...

**Glenn:** A large direct mailing company did a long term survey where they showed only 15% of people buy a product they are interested in, in the first few months. Most, close to 85%, don't buy until 3 - 18 months later. What this means in real estate is often agents write off leads as non-performing way too soon because they didn't buy a house with them in the first month or so. That's looking to the short term.

The number one reason why most agents don't make a lot of money is they are looking at short term money all the time instead of working towards the long term. What they realize is that 85% of the people represent the equity of your business and I always think about it as an oven. I am just going to put them in the oven for the next 3-18 months and they will pop up when they are ready to buy a home or ready to sell a home.

As long as I can just communicate with them, in an orderly manner, and it doesn't mean calling them every day, "Have you decided? Are you ready now?" Why don't we just give them the information and let them buy a home when they are ready or let them sell their home when they are ready. And when you do that its funny because people go, "Oh, you care more about me than yourself right now." That's how you build a high referral-based business. It is just by coming from that service mindset.

**Susan:** How do we stay in touch with them without being overly intrusive?

**Glenn:** The most important thing is to ask their permission. Is it okay for you to stay in touch? If they say no then great, that's fine. You almost want their no's because there are so many people who actually want to do business with you. But, I would just usually say, if I meet them at an open house or I met them somewhere else or they were referred but they are not ready. "I am going to be sending you some relevant real estate information. Is it okay if I get your email address?" Or, simply ask them if they would like a free list of the top 10 best homes for sale. I will talk more about this later on.

Then I could put them into any of the CRM programs I have like Top Producer or Keller Williams has eEdge. There are lots of different programs and they have these things called 33 Touch programs which are basically a series of email drips where you just stay in touch with them. You could also, once a month, send them a "just sold" real estate report. A lot of times people ask, "Hey can you just put me on your MLS automated search program and keep me posted if you see anything?"

What if you could do that but the cool thing I have noticed is, if you send them what is sold about every 2 weeks it is really appreciated, because most of the other agents just send them the new listings coming out. If you can turn your program; and a lot of them are easy to do, and just send them what is sold in the last 2 weeks, it's a really cool thing for them to see because they just think if you keep sending them property all the time there is just more properties coming up all the time. What they don't actually see, that house that came out might have sold.

**Susan:** Right and that house that they really liked on the waterfront is now gone.

**Glenn:** It's gone. Send the solds; in Toronto we call them prospect matches. That's a great way to stay in touch. Every 2 weeks just say, "Hey, thought you'd want to know what sold. Let me know if you have any questions."

**Susan:** I love it.

**Glenn:** What I love to do for our past clients, is about once a year, I film myself at my desk looking on the MLS and going "Hey June, it's Glenn. Just want to let you know in the last 6 months, 5 houses have sold on your street and this is what they sold for. And, there are 3 on the market right now. Just thought you'd want to know that. Take care. Bye."

They love this because I'm not asking them for anything. They say, "Glenn thought of me. He remembered me." Why not? Why wouldn't you want to do it? What I've also understood is that everything we do for the client before the closing transactions is because we are being paid for it. We are on the clock. Anything you do after the transaction you get like triple bonus air miles because people don't expect it.

**Susan:** That's not difficult to do either. In fact, I would imagine, if it's in a rising market, it's actually fun to do. It's validating their purchase all over again and if they were even thinking about moving they would get more exited.

**Glenn:** Yeah and the other thing I noticed, this has been really big in our coaching program, is you just call all of your past clients from the last say 4 to 24 months and just ask them two questions. The first question is, "How are you?" Because a lot of times we are so close with them when we are working with them and all of a sudden it ends. I always would call and say, "Hi, I'm just going through withdrawal symptoms because we haven't talked for the past few months. I just want to know how you are doing." The first question is just how are you doing? The second question is, "How's the home? Is everything okay?" I would argue that you pray that something is wrong.

**Susan:** Really?

**Glenn:** Yes. We find they will often say, "Love it. It's great except there's one toilet." Then you say, "Listen, can I send a plumber out there to address this? It's on me. Let me do it."

**Susan:** I love it.

**Glenn:** That is something where people just go wow and there's this beautiful thing that happens when you call without expectations and you are just coming from contribution and they recognize it. More importantly from a marketing point of view, you get your name back in their head. They start thinking Glenn in real estate and when they're at a party that weekend and they've got your number in their phone, it's amazing how many referrals you'd get. What we did with one of my coaching clients is we asked him to call 38 of his clients. That generated 17 referrals in two weeks for him!

**Susan:** What? That's crazy.

**Glenn:** By simply calling and asking the two questions. It's not do you want to sell your house? It's hi, how are you? Just thinking about you, I miss you. Secondly how's the house? They'll bring up stuff.

**Susan:** Any agent can do that.

**Glenn:** Yeah, it's free. It doesn't cost you anything, but unfortunately on that same NAR study it said that 80% of clients would use their agent again. That's actually how happy they were, only 22% actually do. The reason 80% don't, and only 22% do, is because they didn't keep in touch with the client anymore and they just thought it was, "Because I helped once you will naturally come back to me." That's probably the biggest mistake you can make.

**Susan:** Is there any window, where if too much time is gone by you wouldn't pick up the phone, Glenn?

**Glenn:** I get asked that question a lot and I think and I actually got this idea from Joe Stumpf. He does a thing called the humble apology phone call or letter where he just calls up past clients and says, "You know what? Listen, I'm really sorry. I haven't kept in touch with you for the last two years and I feel terrible about it."

The clients turn around and apologize to you. They are like, "Oh no, don't feel bad. We haven't even kept in touch with you either. We are so sorry. How are you? How are you doing? We are great. Everything is good."

We think after a year or two our clients will hate us. When we actually call and lead with, "I'm really sorry," they say, "No, no, I'm sorry. Glenn, we feel bad. John and I were just talking about that last night." That's really cool.

**Susan:** I love it.

## Why Agents Need to Spend 80% of Their Time Focusing on the next Two Clients Most Likely to Buy or Sell...

**Glenn:** The next thing we are talking about is the 15% that will buy now and 85% long term. What if we just spent 80% of the time working with that 15%? That might only be two clients a month, two clients a week, four clients a month. Right now if agents ask themselves, "Who are the two people that are most likely to convert in the next week or two?" Then you start spending 80% of your time trying to make that happen. Whether you door knock to find them the right property or focus more on MLS or whatever it might be. The moment we started doing that in our coaching program, people started to convert really quickly.

What I've learned is once you start getting a deal or two then you get one, one month then it goes to two the next month and then four the third month, people get a lot more confident and they just get on a roll and then business just starts to fall in your lap.

**Susan:** I love it. That's easy to do too.

## How Agents Hit Their Annual Goals...

**Glenn:** If you want to double your annual income, you can start by doubling your monthly income. It's the easiest sure fire way to do it. If you were doing one transaction a month, just focus on getting two this month. Next month focus on just getting two and just getting two. If you do that you'll actually start doubling your income. What you would actually see is people go from one to two to four to eight.

## Why the 4:1 Ratio of Current Book of Business to Written Transactions Is Key...

**Susan:** Very good. What else in your simple formula can they do?

**Glenn:** A very simple way, if you really want to double your income, is to spend time in your niche market, your income will double or triple because what used to be my favorite client was someone who sold their semi-detached or duplex house. In Toronto that would sell for $600,000 to $800,000 and then they would move up. They would usually move up about 50% to their $800,000 or $1 million house and if I just did that one transaction, I know that would be about $30,000 to $40,000 in commission. If I want to make $200,000 a year, I only have to find five of those people to do it.

That's the beautiful thing about the double your income formula. The most important thing I would add is know that people will move on their own time-frame and I know we talked about it earlier. I always use the thing called the 4:1 ratio which is their current book of business to their current client. If I'm working with 8 people that are looking to buy a home, 2 of them will probably buy that month and 6 won't. We figured out if I'm working with 2, maybe no one will buy that month. If I'm working with 12 probably 3 will buy, that's one quarter.

If you want to do 3 transactions a month, you need to have 12 clients you are working with. Or, if you want to do 2 transactions you need to have 8. What's really cool about this is once those 2 people buy you only have to replace 2 more people.

**Susan:** Why aren't all of them closing? Or if you are working with 12 clients, why doesn't that translate into 12 sales?

**Glenn:** Because life happens. They get separated before they buy the house. They lose their job. Their family member becomes ill. They become ill. They change their mind. Life just happens, that we can't control. If I'm working with 8 clients who are actively looking for a house, on average 2 will convert. Now some months I might get all 8 and I've done that for sure. On average if I wanted to plan my year if I want to do $1 million in real estate sales very month, I need to be working with $4 million worth of clients.

**Susan:** Interesting.

**Glenn:** It's just how it works and I don't know why it happens. It just does. When I track this and I've coached for thousands of agents, it's this formula that we discovered. It just always works with four times as many clients as you need to close each month.

**Susan:** I want to step back and ask what you said about picking a home like going from the $600,000 home to the $1.5 million. Do you recommend that even if an agent isn't used to selling $1.5 million; or do we need to stay within our comfort zone here?

**Glenn:** For best results I would probably stay within your comfort zone. I totally understand why agents would feel that way because in the beginning when I was selling homes for $100,000, I would get the shakes if someone wanted to buy a house for $300,000 because I just didn't think I was qualified. When I was selling houses for $500,000 and someone wanted to buy a place for a million, I was like, "Oh my God, that's so weird." What I have learned is it is actually easier to sell a $2 million house than it is to sell an $85,000 house.

**Susan:** Why is that?

**Glenn:** The people who are buying and selling $ 2,000,000 houses are pretty good decision makers in their careers so they have been promoted through their company or built their business or their lawyers or whatever. They make high quality decisions and that's why they have risen so high. Secondly, they make a lot of money so your fee isn't a big deal to them. They actually make more per hour than you do. When I sell a cheaper house I often will make more money than they do and they are like, they don't feel good about it.

**Susan:** Do you find the higher end homes don't fall out because the buyer can't qualify as much and things like that?

**Glenn:** That's right and at the lower end it's going to happen. They are also harder to put together. I can't tell you the amount of times it's been 2:00 in the morning and we are arguing about the microwave that's 11 years old out of principle. I am not in judgment about that at all, it's just because that's what it is.

I find at the higher end of the spectrum, they look at homes between $2 and $5 million. They have more flexibility and the seller and the buyer still both want it as quick as they can and as much as they can. But I just find those transactions can be put together easier if you are working with really great clients.

**Susan:** Interesting.

**Glenn:** My recommendation would be start in whatever single niche market you feel most comfortable with; if you like working with dog owners who have a Golden Retriever, then join the Golden Retriever club. Get to know those people and if it's young professionals, join that club or if it's doing first time buyers seminars because you just want to work with first time buyers.

You work in whatever market you feel most comfortable with and if you want to help people who like Golden Retrievers then that's a great single niche target market for you. If you like people who want to buy in a great school district or they want to sell and move, that's perfect too. If you just want to work in open houses that is fine. We have agents at our brokerage that make hundreds of thousands of dollars a year because they have mastered open houses.

If we want to go a bit deeper on this, if you said to me, "Well Glenn, my niche market is open houses in a certain area." I would say to you, "If that's what you want to do and you love meeting at open houses, let's just make that so spectacular that it provides all the income you will ever need." The first way you can do it is to start doing open houses during the week from 4 to 7 pm. There is no rule that says they have to be on the weekend and if you are not doing anything because it's a bit of dead time for most agents, between 4 to 6 - go do open houses.

## The Secret to Successful Open Houses...

Here is the secret, you get your sign out that says, "Open House" and the second sign you put out says, "Neighborhood Real Estate Information Center" and you put a bunch of balloons on it. You see the car slow down and you start to really get excited because they might stop because no one has been in there the whole day. You are like a little dog at the window and then it kind of speeds off, you are like, "Oh." But when I put the $2^{nd}$ sign out, then I realize people aren't just looking at that house. I have now turned this open house into a retail store and people can come in and talk about any house in the neighborhood because it's the free neighborhood real estate information center.

**Susan:** Very good.

**Glenn:** Love that, the other thing I really like is, I encourage a lot of our agents to do the sneak peek open houses. Now boards have different rules, some are: once the listing is on, it must be shown, others you can delay it even though it is listed. On our board, once it's on the real estate board, it has to be available for everyone to show. What I like to do is, I like to bring out the listing late Thursday evening and on the Monday before, I deliver 100 post cards, 50 to homes across the street and 25 on either side inviting them to the sneak peek neighbors only special VIP preview of this property. I say, "Here is your chance to beat other agents and buyers to this home. We are having a wine and cheese tasting on Thursday night from 7 to 9 pm; feel free to come by. You must bring this invitation to get in." We'll get anywhere from 8 neighbors to 80 neighbors who will actually come and it becomes a party.

I like to have fun with it because people will walk up the street carrying this invitation above their head, like they got the VIP. When they come to the door I say, "Do you have the invitation there," and they say, "Yes." "Oh, okay well you can come in." If they don't, it is so funny because I will say, "Oh, this is for VIPs only or neighbors." Inevitably I've so many people in the house, it's like a kitchen party and someone will say, "Oh that's Jones from down the street." I say, "Okay we will let you in." What I do on the wine and cheese is I get four bottles of white wine, four bottles of red wine, a case of water, plated cheese, it's about $140. Then I get my laptop and my projector and I put that up in the dining room to help do MLS searches for them.

It just becomes a house party and I get to meet everyone and I can find out who's moving. This really helps if you are in an area that you don't usually service so then I actually find out, "Oh what's your favorite school?" They will tell you all about it and what they like about the area and everything and it's really great. That builds it up for the weekend open house because then they can go and tell their friends and colleagues and so I get a bigger showing at the Saturday and Sunday open house.

**Susan:** I've heard open houses don't sell houses. You are saying it does help sell the house? They aren't just about getting clients for the agent holding it open?

**Glenn:** It does both. It builds up activity. I get to meet all the neighbors so I easily pick up more business. They will tell me someone is moving into the area or they might be moving or they will say, "Can we talk afterwards?" They will say stuff like that. But more importantly they will bring their kids back or colleagues back on the weekend because they got the sneak peek. You have these huge turn outs for your open house. I know one agent who started 10 years ago, brand new, and is now up to over 500 transactions a year and just only does open houses. She started doing one on Saturday and one on Sunday. Then she went up to doing three on Saturday, three on Sunday. So she would do 11 to 1, 1 to 3, 3 to 5 at different houses and then move because she just knew that's where all the leads would be coming from.

**Susan:** Are these her listings?

**Glenn:** They could have been or could not have. A lot of times in our office and in other offices, people are looking for people to cover their open houses. I say, "Great, yeah I will go and do it." When they come into the open house you obviously show them the home, you are trying to sell the home for the seller that's what you are hired for. What if you could give them a free offer? Dean Jackson came up with this idea; asked them if they want a free list of the top ten homes for sale in the neighborhood. Everyone wants that list usually if that's what they are after and when they say, "Yeah, I would love the list," and then I just say, "Well I want to send you the right list."

## Why Offering a Free Orientation Tour Works...

I ask them four key questions directly from every buyer consultation which are: What is the perfect area you're looking in? What does the perfect home look like? What's the perfect time frame? What's the perfect price? Based on their answers I can hand pick and send them the ten best homes. Then when I send it to them and they reply, I can offer to bring them out on a free orientation tour. We are going to see six or eight homes. You are not allowed to buy a home that day. Its free, first one is on me, let's go and do it. It's easy the easier you make it for people to do business with you. It's amazing how much business you get.

**Susan:** What is a free orientation tour?

**Glenn:** What I offered people is if they want this free list instead of making them come in for a buyer consultation like all the other agents do and make them sign a buyer agreement and they have to come into my office and all that garbage. I just say I am going to email you the list after the open house. I am going to go back on the computer based on what you told me about perfect price, perfect home, perfect location and perfect time frame. I am going to send you my top ten picks and then when I send them that list, as a courtesy, what we do is we offer a free orientation tour of those homes.

We'll see five to ten of those homes in two hours. You are not allowed to buy a home that day. We are just going to go out and see what you are looking for. Then what I do in the first home I show them I spend

45 minutes and I really give them a complete education on it. Okay this is what a wet basement looks like if they have basements. This is what mold looks like. This furnace is full. These windows are old. The hardwood floors are that. I tell them all the costs that are going to be associated with them buying that house. After that first house most of them all would say the same thing they'll go, "Oh my god Glenn I'm so happy I'm working with you."

**Susan:** Do you pick a sort of "bad" first house?

**Glenn:** Sometimes yeah, if it's a vacant house that needs lots of work, it's much easier to point out more deficiency right? Though it's not always picking the worst house to set them up, it's more like okay I'd rather show you the raw material first.

That's going to get them educated and then it just follows along. Like that's all I want to do, make it so ridiculously easy for them to do business with me. They'll do business with me and tell all their friends, "This guy is so easy to do business with."

**Susan:** Right, you wouldn't make your best friend come in and sign an agency disclosure.

**Glenn:** No.

**Susan:** You would meet him in the house and say, "Let's take a look."

**Glenn:** That's right. Let's go and look at houses. You can't buy one that day. That's what I tell my best friend. Some people will go, "Oh come on if I find a house, Glenn, could I buy it?" I say "No." They say, "Come on." I say, "Okay. If you really want to buy it you can. But the whole point really is just to go and see if what you are looking for and your price expectations are where you want. If they are at the same level, and if they are not that's okay we are going to figure it out." For most people their price is in the middle but their expectations are way higher.

We just have to be able to either adjust your price or adjust your expectations. That's all there is to it. We are not going into that until we go and see five or six houses and then you tell me what you like and what you don't like. Then I can tell you. You might not even have to spend that much on a house. Or you might have to spend a little bit more or we need to go out a few more times and make sure we find you a great place.

**Susan:** I love it.

**Glenn:** I just want to make it the easy button for everyone to do real estate with me. They always say, "That was so easy to do business." I think if you want to double your income, that's exactly what you need to do.

# How to Use Geographic Farming to Double Your Income...

**Susan:** What else do they need to know Glenn?

**Glenn:** Let's talk about geographic farming. One of the things that I would do is calculate what the turnover is in the neighborhood. There are 500 homes and there are 50 sales in a given year that gives me a turnover rate of 10%.

I'm always looking for an area with a turnover rate of at least 8% to 14%. This is the big mistake most people make when they pick an area, because they'll try to pick a luxury home or established larger homes. We found that for people between 42 and 65 it's a very low turnover. They are building their family. They are getting their kids to school. They are not moving. It's the turnover rate I'm looking for. If I was going to start and you dropped me in any city in the United States or Canada, and said, "Glenn you've got to make $100, 000 in the next 100 days." The first thing I would do is go find where all the first time buyers buy their first home. Where are the first time sellers? They are usually in town houses or in condominiums in big cities or they are in smaller detached homes. You probably know them in your area where people just turnover all the time.

**Susan:** Absolutely.

**Glenn:** I'm going to pick the area with the highest turnover first. Then I'm going to do some research. I'm going to go back two years to see where all the sellers moved to. One of the ways I can do that is I can probably put their name into like a 411.ca or some online search tool. It will tell me where they've moved to. Then I'm going to start finding patterns; like most people sell at West Point here and they move over to this area. It's because the homes are bigger, it's got a better school, and it's a better area.

Then I'm going to start doing some marketing. First of all I'm going to go and door knock to the people who are in the high turnover area. What I would say to them is most people right now like yourself, who we know are 80% first time buyers, sell within five years. You are probably sitting around the table thinking should we renovate this place? Should we finish our basement? Should we renovate the kitchen? Or should we move to a larger home? If you want to renovate your basement or do any fix ups and just stay here, I have lots of contractors that I happily refer people to. No fee, it's just what I do.

If you are thinking about moving, we find a lot of people in this area are moving over here. What we offer is a free list of the top ten best homes in that neighborhood and we also have a free orientation tour. All I'm working on is their purchase not on their sale. Does that make sense?

Most people aren't sellers until they are buyers. Though they might talk about selling but until they actually go out there and buy then they move. If you ever notice people will say, "Oh, we are just looking, just thinking, just looking, not sure, just thinking." Then something happens, they shift and go into overdrive looking on the weekend or something.

**Susan:** Right.

**Glenn:** They go out and walk through an open house and they find a house. If this happens, I want to be the person they call if they find a house.

The other thing is if I want to find buyers for that home that they are selling I can go on Craigslist or Kijiji. I could go to where the renters are and I could start marketing to them a free list of the top ten best homes in West Point. Now I can actually start building up this ten people who are thinking about buying in West Point. Then I've got 10 people in West Point who are thinking about selling and moving. Now I've got what we call, "complementary neighborhoods." Then I can start to play this game or I can almost create my own MLS system. I've got all the buyers and the sellers and I know where they are going.

**Susan:** Fascinating. How do you get the sellers to tell you where they are moving to, if they haven't started to move?

**Glenn:** By doing some research on MLS. They give you the seller's last name. Then you put the sellers last name into a search and you can Google them. Or go to 411.com or whatever. You can use Find My Number.com and if you put in their name a lot of times because all the phone companies share this data, you'll find where they moved to. Or the other way is you can go on MLS and see which agent they used and then where were the homes that that agent sold next? It takes a little bit of work.

Or simply knock on their door and ask them if they were to move where would they go next? I know at least 15 or 20 of these people are moving in the next 12 months. I want to be the first who gets three or four or five of them. Then when I get my first listing, I'm going to sneak peak open house and invite all the rest of the neighbors over. I'm going to get them there and now I can start to build my own geographic farm.

## How to Take the Stress and Worry Out of Real Estate...

**Susan:** Very well said, I love this.

**Glenn:** There are different formulas for each niche market. I guess my whole point of this book is just find one that you would love to wake up to every day. Be happy or work with that client or that type of house in that area. Making hopefully your largest paycheck and all of a sudden real estate becomes a really fun game instead of a whole lot of stress and worry.

**Susan:** Do your agents have success with social media?

**Glenn:** We've got some agents who do quite well on some of the social media platforms, if they are really good at it and they are consistent. I've seen some agents do terrible jobs on there. I've seen agents do really great with straight out internet regeneration where they are spending $500 a month. They are getting leads from a conglomerator who basically just sends 20, 30, 40, 50 leads a month. Then they become masters of converting those leads. The best practice I've seen is it's the person who responds to the lead, the quickest wins. That lead is expecting a response within five or 10 minutes and if you are not willing to do it you might not want to go down that path of internet regeneration.

If you can't do it, have somebody who can do it and hire somebody. Once you start to double your income, you can actually hire somebody to do all this posting and to respond. You can hire other agents, who respond to the leads and book appointments for you. The business becomes way easier when you start to spend all of your time on the 80% of the job you do your best. The other stuff is just stuff like I can sell out listing but I can hire somebody who loves to do it.

I can bring a transaction to closing or I can hire someone who loves to do it. Why are we robbing them of their job which they love to do all the time because we are trying to do everything.

**Susan:** Yeah I love this because you are giving the agent lots of options. If you are someone who thrives in an open house environment, great go do those. For some agents just the thought of sitting at an open house is not appealing at all. That's never going to work for them. But if they are someone who is a little bit more advanced and wants to do the technology leads, they can focus on that. You are giving them lots of different choices to fit their personality. There isn't one solution here. There's actually many to choose from.

**Glenn:** I have all my agents do a D.I.S.C behavioral profile which includes something called the A.VA (Activity Vector Analysis). I have their psychological profile report. I also ask them to read a book by Dan Sullivan called "Unique Ability." It's a really great book. If you read the first two chapters, it tells you all how to find out your unique abilities. You've got to send an email to 15 of your friends saying, "What do you think my unique ability is?" They tell you. Then

I'm coaching them in whatever they love to do all the time. When you specialize, you stay working with people you love to work with instead of running around with everyone. The formula is simple. Find out who you are as an agent, establish your unique ability, then find out who you want to work with, and the area you like to work in.

I've done it before. I've worked with people that I didn't want to work with in areas I didn't want to work, running back and forth, took a listing an hour away. I had to do 50 open houses. It was a money loser. It was not fun. We've all been there. That's why I think this is the simple way to double your income in real estate. If you can be who you are and bring your natural gift of who you want to be with, then we match you up with those people. It's so easy, it's ridiculous.

**Susan:** Yeah and it's like slow down and be a little bit strategic about it is what I think I hear you are saying. We just rush from lead to lead and you are saying, "Hey why don't we sit back a little bit and look at the bigger picture here?"

**Glenn:** If you just slow down, and figure out what you are really good at. If you think about it, that's the way the rest of the world operates. Mick Jagger is great at singing but he's not that good at driving the truck between concerts. He hires people to set the lights and drive the truck right? If you look at anyone who makes a lot of money, they usually do one thing really well and it's in their unique ability. If you look at other people who try to do everything, they are the people who are most stressed out because a lot of what they have to do, they don't enjoy doing.

There's nothing like when I come to work and I'm coaching agents all day because that's my unique ability. I have more energy than anything in the world. I don't love it when I have to come and figure out legal issues or legal contracts or accounting issues. I'm like yeah I can do it, I own these companies but to me it's just stuff. I just choose to spend 80% of my time on what I really like to do. I hire people to do everything else. I'm still involved but I'm just trying to hit my schedule 80% of the time. I know if I do that then I'm perfect. I'm fine.

**Susan:** Very good.

## Why Agents Should Spend 80% of Their Time Doing What They Love…

**Glenn:** I think if agents can just learn to spend 80% of their time doing what they love to do in this business and meeting and working with people, then it becomes much easier.

**Susan:** Right, it's almost like enough success so that they can afford to pay someone to do the parts they aren't as good at or don't enjoy.

**Glenn:** Yeah on my team, 97% of the time my team does the showing and it's very rare that I'll ever do a showing. What I do is the initial consultation with the buyer or with the seller and I'll set the strategy. Then what I do is I'll send them to my buyer's specialist, I don't call him a buyer assistant. It's a buyer specialist because they are better at it than I am and honestly I can't be everywhere. My buyer's specialists, she's like a dog with a bone, right? You tell her what you are looking for and she will go and find it and I don't know how she does it, she just does it.

Me, if I've seen 100,000 houses I don't need to see another one in my life and I'm complete. How many times can you go there and go, "Oh my god that's nice oh yeah. You should get rid of that carpet." "Oh I know it's terrible." I know what I'm good at and even what I did on my team, and I've almost stopped doing that now, I would say this person is going to find that perfect dream home for you and then when they do I'm going to make sure that it's the right home. Then I'll do the negotiations to make sure you are safe then all I have to do is meet somebody to do the negotiations.

**Susan:** I love it.

**Glenn:** Now my clients say, "Glenn we really we don't want to work with you, we are quite happy with her." I say, "Yeah." I call my buyer specialist, "You sure you don't need me?" and she says, "No we are good." Then I say, "Okay." It's all good.

# The Mistakes to Avoid When Trying To Double Your Income…

**Susan:** Are there mistakes that you've seen agents make that they should be on the lookout for?

**Glenn:** My number one would be, stop being a generalist and just chose to be a specialist. That's the biggest thing I can tell you. Number two is, don't pick a broker because they have the lowest fees or the biggest name. You pick a broker whom you think you can rely to do the appropriate training for you. I would also stop trying to convert everybody. Stop trying to do all the same level of service to 4 or 5, 10 or 25 or 30 of your clients. Only 15% of them really need the 80% of your focus right now.

We are going to keep the others in the "oven" and we can maybe touch base with them once a week. What I find the big mistake most agents make is some of these people say, "Wow! We are just looking right now." They start plaguing them all the time and calling them and they are saying, "We already told you we are not in a hurry." Let people buy a home on their own time schedule.

Be there when they need you because they'll move from not looking to like go into 'heat' really quickly and then they'll need to go buy the house. Stop bugging people. Just ask them what they need and give it to them in a very timely way and it's okay to check in every couple of weeks with those people even by email and say, "Just wanted to have a check if everything is still cool, we are still on track where you are moving next spring. Is there anything you need to do?" That's just respecting their time frame, that's what I would say.

Another way to look at this is what if you were super crazy busy writing deals. Would you have time to constantly bug the people who are not yet in a hurry? Of course not, you would be grateful they are not doing anything so you could spend more time with your "hot" clients.

**Susan:** Very good.

**Glenn:** Stop trying to get people to work on your terms all the time. What I mean by that is, this whole notion of I have to prequalify somebody in five minutes or I am not going to waste time with them, is ridiculous. Even if they are not ready they know people who are ready. Well there might be some other trainers who are like, "No, no, no. Close, close, close," all the time. I think that works if that's your personality, then do that but most people don't operate that way. I don't walk into a grocery store and have the cashier closing in on what I am purchasing as soon as I walk in; they let me browse. When I am ready to get to the cashier I will show up and buy my stuff they don't have to sell me anything in the grocery store.

Stop trying to get people to sign buyer agency agreements the moment you meet them. Stop trying to use open house registry because the seller told you they wanted them, for "security reasons." In 25 years I have never had a seller ever say, "For security reasons, could you ask for everyone's driver's license." I have for sure seen a lot of sales trainers tell you that's the way to get everyone's name. Well that's how to get their name if you want it, but when will you follow up with them? Yes maybe it works for sometimes but most are frankly annoyed because you told them, you needed the name for security reasons, not that you were going to be following up with them.

Stop bugging people, you should be offering them great product services so they want to give you their name. Like who wouldn't want the free list of the top ten best homes? Who wouldn't want to go on a free orientation tour? Offer them two free orientation tours, like, "The first two are on me," even if you never buy a house, ever in your life. The more you like push somebody away and you say, "No it's okay. I will do everything for you," the more they start to audition to become your customer. It's like when I was dating the more hard-to-get you played…

**Susan:** I love it.

**Glenn:** Just remember to treat all of your clients as your best friend until they prove otherwise. Just show up, be great, and tell them what you are going to do. Actually do it on a proper time line, treat them like you're the best friend ever and they will show up as your best friend ever and they will become your best clients ever and send you lots of people. A referral is really sending someone you care about to someone you trust, and the bottom line too is it makes them feel good when they get to refer great service just as I feel great when I get to refer a great restaurant to you or anyone else.

## What Sellers Really Want from A Real Estate Agent...

Just wanted to share a few more interesting items from the NAR Profile of Home Buyers and Sellers.

### How Sellers found their agent?
1. Referred by Friend, neighbor or relative 39%
2. Used agent previously to buy or sell home 22%
3. Referred through employer or Relocation Company 5%
4. Prospecting efforts of agent 4%
5. Saw open house or For Sale sign 4%
6. Visited open house and met agent 4%
7. Referred by another agent 4%
8. Internet / website 3%
9. Direct mail
10. Walked into Real Estate office 1%

### Number of agents contacted before selecting one to assist with sale of home
66% - contacted only one agent
16% - contacted / met with two agents
13% - met / contacted three agents
3% - met / contacted four agents
2% - contacted 5 or more

### What sellers want the most from Real Estate Agents by level of service provided by Agent
1. Help Seller market home to potential buyers 24%
2. Help price home competitively 20%
3. Help sell within specific time frame 19%
4. Help find buyer for home 19%
5. Help Seller find ways to fix up and stage home 9%
6. Help with price negotiations 5%
7. Help with paperwork 3%

**Most important factor when choosing a Real Estate Agent**
1. Reputation of agent 38%
2. Agent is honest and trustworthy 20%
3. Agent is friend or family member 18%
4. Agent's knowledge of the neighborhood 11%
5. Agent's association with a particular firm 5%
6. Agent has caring personality/good listener 4%
7. Professional designations held by agent 1%

The research shows that Sellers want to work with a Realtor that they already know, were referred to, or worked with previously. They also want to work with an agent that is honest, trustworthy, knowledgeable, and is a good listener. They do not really care which company their Realtor works for, as they choose agents… not companies.

The world would be a better place if our colleagues understood what Buyers and Sellers really want from a Real Estate Agent. Then, they seek out and learn the proper skills, knowledge and training, in order to deliver this at a really high level.

# What Buyers Really Want from A Real Estate Agent...

I encourage you to visit the NAR site and buy the full report... but here are some interesting highlights:

## What Buyers want from a Real Estate Agent
55% - Help find the right home for them
13% - Help with price negotiations
12% - Help negotiate the other terms of the sale
7% - Show them what other comparables sold for
6% - Help with the paperwork
3% - Determine how much they can afford

## How Buyers found their agent
41% - were referred by a relative, friend or colleague
12% - Internet / Website
8% - met agent at public open house
6% - for sale sign
5% - were referred by another Realtor
4% - Relocation Company
3% - contacted through Realtor prospecting

## Most important factors when choosing a Real Estate Agent
30% - picked agent because they were honest and trustworthy
20% - reputation of agent
15% - agent was friend or family member
14% - knowledge of neighbourhood
13% - Agent was good listener and had a caring personality
3% - Agent's association with particular firm

# How to Turn 1 Listing into 4 Additional Transactions...

**Glenn:** I love listings! And so do all of the top agents.

We all understand that our goal is to get the most money for the Sellers, as quickly as possible and with the fewest problems. This is the universal goal of all top listing Agents. What if we were to be a bit more strategic, and focus on picking up a minimum of three more transactions for every new listing we take?

**Let's start with getting the Listing first**

If I lead generate and get one listing appointment from one of these 8 sources:

1. Sphere of Influence
2. Farm area
3. Craigslist, Kijiji, Facebook or other Social media/marketing
4. FSBO'S
5. Referrals from past clients or friends
6. Targeted door knocking in high turnover areas
7. People I meet throughout the day
8. Other Realtor's across the country and the U.S.

**I can then start to "vertically market" around that listing. For example, if I have a listing appointment in a "move-up" area...**

1. I could start a marketing campaign to the people living in their first home that are most likely to move to this neighbourhood. The easiest way to find out these patterns is to go through all of the recent sales

in the "First-time" seller neighbourhoods over the past 2 years, enter the Sellers name in 411.ca and see where they have moved to. The patterns will become very clear.

2. I could also call all of my past clients who live in that area.

3. I could market either the listing (if I have it) or the fact that there will be a new listing coming out on either Craigslist or Kijiji, and generate leads from potential move-up Buyers. **I could advertise the monthly carrying costs on the "Looking to rent: or "Homes for rent" sections of these sites as well!**

4. I hold a neighbours only sneak-peek open house before the listing comes onto the market and generate $2 - $3,000,000 in new business.

5. I could approach FSBO's in the "first time seller" neighbourhood to see if they would like to come and see my new listing.

6. I could go "upstream" and lead generate in the market where my seller is moving to…

7. I could place an ad on Craigslist or Kijiji and target the area that my Sellers are moving to.

8. I could go and door-knock the First-time Seller neighbourhood and tell them about my new listing.

9. I could market via flyers or postcards to the upstream market (see #6)

10. I could hold an open house on the weekend to pick up 2-3 more Buyers or Sellers. Start holding open houses during the week between 4 – 7:00pm. Just add an additional sign that says "Neighbourhood Real Estate Information Centre."

There are at least 7 easy additional transactions from every Listing we take. Your job is to get at least 3-4 of them. You could:

1)  Find the Buyer for your Listing
2)  Find a Buyer for another home in the area
3)  Get another Listing on the same street
4)  Get another Listing in the neighbourhood
5)  Find the seller another home
6)  Sell the Listing of Buyer who bought your listing
7)  Get a Referral from the Seller

So, focus on the additional transactions you can get from every new Listing you take!!

The great thing about following the "vertical marketing" strategy is that for every new lead, Listing and Buyer that you meet...simply "rinse, lather and repeat" this strategy, and you will be well on your way to making 2015, your best year ever.

## How to Get More Referrals from "Referral Chaining"...

The beauty of Referral Chaining is to get more referrals from your Sphere of Influence.

I have found one of the best ways to get more referrals is to simply go back and thank the person who sent you a referral. It makes them feel good, and they will probably send you another referral.

The really cool way to get more referrals is to look back at the person who referred the person who just referred you! For example, when I did this I noticed some of the chains of referrals were 25 people long! Let's use a simpler example to illustrate the benefits of Referral Chaining.

Bob refers Mary to you. So you call back Bob and say thank you so much for referring Mary to me. What if Bob was referred by Peter originally? After your call to Bob, simply pick up the phone and call Peter. When Peter answers say this "Peter, it's Glenn, how are you?" Then say, "Peter, remember when you referred Bob to me and I found him a great home?" Peter says "Of course." Then you say, "Well, Bob just referred me to his friend Mary! So I wanted to just call and thank you because none of this would have happened without you introducing me to Bob, Thanks again and have a great day."

Now Peter feels great too...and you will probably get a referral from Peter in the next couple of days.

So make a list of all of your past referrals in the last 24 months and then simply remember where the referral came from, and start Referral Chaining your way to success.

## Start Selling Real Estate for the "Hugs"...

One of the best parts of a career in Real Estate is the "Hugs" we receive from our clients. You know the moment when you told the Buyers that their offer has been accepted, or the Sellers, that their home is finally sold. It is the magical moment of every transaction and the fuel that keeps us coming back for more.

It's funny, that in our industry we spend so much time talking about "deals" and the number of Listings we took. Many training programs focus on selling "houses", handling objections, and close, close, close. The reality is that we don't sell houses; we find homes for people to build a great future for themselves and their family.

We are responsible for advising them and keeping them safe as they navigate the dream of home ownership. While many of our conversations are transactional in nature i.e. number of bedrooms, baths, garage spaces, big yard, small yard or layout and view from their condominium...the essence of what we do is purely emotional.

Our job is to help our clients create the best life possible for them and their family. What people really buy is a great school district, a better life for their children, walking distance to great shops, restaurants, transit, parks or access to highways for their commute.

The most successful agents in this business generally have a repeat and referral based business that generates at least 80% of their volume. By definition, a referral is sending someone you care about to someone you trust. It is actually an emotional referral. People will come back to you time and time again because you care, not because they felt they were just another deal to you.

They come back, and also send everyone they know to you because of the "hugs' and the emotional bonding that occurred throughout the transaction. I see it all a bit melancholy. They are happy and excited about their new home, but sad that they won't get to have us in their daily lives….and we feel exactly the same way.

I love real estate when I get to deal with clients who are raving fans of my business. I love working with people who know what they want, are reasonable, open to advice and consulting and are appreciative. They get the biggest 'hugs" from me.

Our goal should be to eliminate all of the people we deal with who live in a world of greed, envy and unethical behaviour. Refer them to your competition as soon as possible and gum up their business. They don't like "hugs" anyway…

So, start selling Real Estate for hugs! It will change your business and your life, when you surround yourself with great people. More importantly, it will make you feel like you are making a difference in people's lives and living your life on purpose. It is truly a win/win situation.

# Here's How to Double Your Income While Working Less...

**Susan:** Glenn, thank you for this. This has actually been very educational because I think a lot of agents do think that they will get their license and the phone will just ring and this isn't necessarily the case. Thank you for sharing your wisdom with us because I found there is nothing you shared with us today that says, "Get out a check and write a big check for $10,000 so you can make a $100,000."

**Glenn:** It's all about just show up, learn to work your target market, show up as a great best friend and human being, with great integrity and people will line up. The world doesn't need more agents but they do need more great agents and if we can create more great agents and get rid of all the not so great agents, I think we can do a great service for everyone in our industry.

You already know how to work with buyers and sellers and close deals in real estate. The confusing part is not knowing the proven formula successful agents use to earn 6 and 7 figures consistently so your income is predictable.

That's where we come in. We help people just like you double your real estate income while working less, not more.

**Step 1:** We work with you to identify your unique ability. What are you better at than anyone else? Once we know this we can then leverage your unique talents for more income.

**Step 2:** We help you identify your ideal single target market so you can work with the clients you love most and cash more and larger commission checks.

**Step 3:** We then work with you ongoing by giving you the scripts and the blueprint to go really deep in your market, think neighborhood domination, not dabbling.

Most agents think it takes years of hard work and hours sitting open houses to earn a good living in real estate.

Now you can double your income and work less if you want to.

**Susan:** If they have any questions how can they get in touch with you?

**Glenn:** They can:

1. email me at: glennmcqueenie@gmail.com
2. Join my weekly podcast by calling: 1-866-561-7445
3. Join my webinar at: doubleyourincomeforagents.com
4. Join me for a 2-day workshop at: www.doubleyourincomeexperience.com

## About the Author

Until he graduated from University, Glenn McQueenie worked in 27 different jobs starting at the age of 10. As a result of all those different jobs and bosses, he made the decision that he never wanted to work for any employer ever again. In 1989 he got his Real Estate License and never looked back. Glenn spent the early part of his career in real estate in the trenches showing over 100,000 homes and helping thousands of people Buy and Sell Real Estate. Glenn also helped most of the Toronto Blue Jays baseball team find their homes in Toronto from 1999-2003, prior to opening his own Brokerage in 2004.

Glenn has been fortunate to seek out great teachers, coaches and Mentors in his Real Estate career and has spent over $1,000,000 of his own money attending great training and coaching all over the globe. Glenn is passionate about sharing the insights and wisdom he's gleaned with other agents so they too can be successful. Glenn is committed to helping agents gain the skills, knowledge, confidence, energy and momentum they need to live an abundant life...and loves when he sees them inspired to in turn start giving back to others.

Glenn opened his first Real Estate Brokerage office in Toronto in 2004, and now has over 300 associates with the launch of his second office last year in Downtown Toronto. This is a result of bringing great agents together for great training and mentoring. Glenn is currently running a pilot program called "Double Your Income" Coaching Program in his offices, which has given him additional insight for this book.

Glenn gets his greatest joy when he hears back from agents about their successes, after implementing one of the techniques they have just learned in the program. Glenn is committed to building an army of educated, successful and profitable agents, who have a life worth living and give back to the community at a really high level.

Glenn Lives in Toronto with his wife Janet, two teenage kids, and an overly friendly Golden Retriever named Marlowe.

www.ingramcontent.com/pod-product-compliance
Lightning Source LLC
Chambersburg PA
CBHW071805170526
45167CB00003B/1183